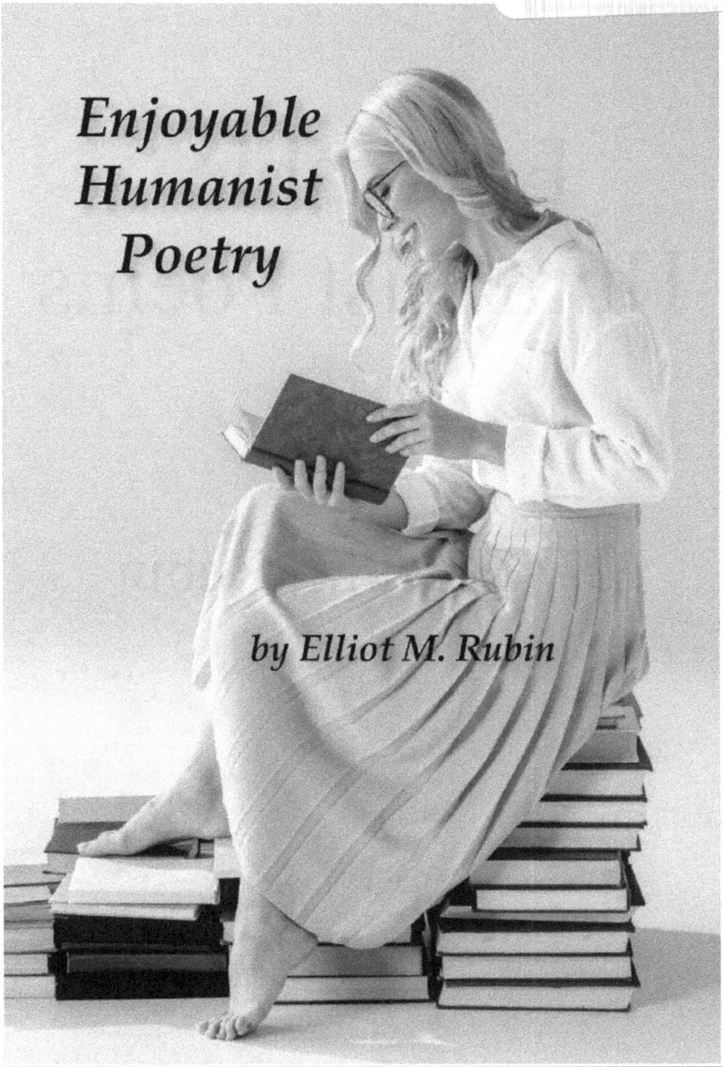

# Enjoyable Humanist Poetry

### by Elliot M. Rubin

# Enjoyable Humanist Poems

By Elliot M. Rubin

Copyright January 2020
Library of Congress


ISBN 978-1-7328493-4-1


No part of this book may be reproduced in any form whatsoever without the prior express written consent of the author.

This book is fiction, and all names, people, places, and happenings are from the author's imagination and are used fictionally.

Any resemblance to any living or dead persons and/or businesses, locations, and/or events are coincidental in its entirety.

All rights reserved

**Dedication**
To my grandchildren
Shane, Isabelle, Jonathan, Carter,
Alexandra, Melanie, Mollie, and Madison

**In Memory of**
Herman S. Rubin
Who wrote poetry all his life.

**Preface**

Poetry is to be read and understood. To be written in plain English for everyone's enjoyment. Too often, poets write in-depth, penetrating poems where you need to be well-read and versed in the nuances of literature to appreciate the poetry, not this book or any of my writings.

## Table of Contents

a walk at night ................................................................8
facing reality................................................................10
flight ...........................................................................11
a poetic reality ............................................................12
immortal thoughts ......................................................13
the last conversation ..................................................14
tragedy today .............................................................15
thinking .....................................................................16
America, the best country in the world......................18
forgiveness ................................................................19
waiting for tomorrow ..................................................20
desire .........................................................................21
dreaming....................................................................22
first time i saw you ....................................................23
real people .................................................................24
Susan .........................................................................25
Susan's sister.............................................................26
at the library ..............................................................27
eggs ...........................................................................28
confusion ...................................................................29
her...............................................................................30
goodbye ......................................................................31
replaying life ..............................................................32
undying love ...............................................................33
karma..........................................................................34
fidelity ........................................................................35

| | |
|---|---|
| the gift | 36 |
| God | 37 |
| winter day in the cemetery | 38 |
| happy new year | 39 |
| the big question | 40 |
| the waitress | 41 |
| *give me your tired, your poor* | 42 |
| rain | 43 |
| missing but here | 44 |
| sheep | 45 |
| flight to Las Vegas | 46 |
| Pearl | 47 |
| music | 48 |
| the tree in my yard | 49 |
| humanity | 50 |
| my muse | 51 |
| driving to work | 52 |
| common emotions | 53 |
| finally, love | 54 |
| suicide | 55 |

**a walk at night**

'twas midnight black as pitch,
no one near, muscles twitch,
clutching my phone ever so tight,
my nerves rattle, from ghostly fright

i enter through the rust-covered gate,
creaking loud, i decide to wait-
i look around at many small mounds
scattered all about on silent still grounds

the full moon tonight is at its height,
as church bells sound, so out of breath
slowly once, twice, until all twelve
break the silence, of eternal death

echoes of silence
  broken twelve times
    waking the dead
      from endless sleep

a dark shadow sits high
watching the dead,
then looks at me, to turn its head,
giving a black cat's, sly eye

i see massive stones, rigid as troops,
waiting for orders, not moving at all-
i see in the distance, in the night,
a line of barren trees, lonely and tall

they wait for a storm, hard and severe,
to be uprooted, no one sheds a tear
when they fall, to join the dead below;
another death, another life to flow-
their trunks are hollow, eaten by bugs
who travel up, from the graves so low

shadows drift up, from a field not far,
gathering merrily, as in a bar,
gliding in the air, at a newly dug grave
where i stand; frozen in fear-
calling out, they disappear,
as if, never here

a short walk, to where they prance
are shadows with eyes, ever so bright,
filling my soul, with deathly fright-
yet i stand, in a cemetery at night,
where souls rise, to merrily dance

i see a plot, not yet marked,
except for soldier's wreath, laid on top-
dead and buried, unknown to all,
except by those predeceased, and on-call

welcomed him home, at midnight tonight,
lonely no more, with old friends now found,
finally honored, on hallowed ground,
remembered by all, who fell before

**facing reality**

the yellow fields of summer wheat
stand tall and fertile with seeds,
are now covered in winter's blanket
with white frozen morning dew

the season's pages turn
reminds me as i walk by,
i age with every small step
acknowledging my mortality

**flight**

no longer crawling caterpillars,
butterflies flit
from flower to flower,
the sun reflects off
fluttering multicolored wings;
ever so elegant
in the midsummer morning air

jealous of their beauty,
the ability to soar,
my aged body
no longer agile,
arthritis racked,
only my mind
still young

the end of creativity,
end of my being
looms over the horizon

need to soar
like the butterflies-
adrenaline pulsating
for one last time,
like Thelma and Louise
breathing in a final rush of air

**a poetic reality**

a poet writes poetry is
like a gigolo chasing girls

the visceral thrill
to achieve goals
drives both
in their endeavors

**immortal thoughts**

my body is finite
it'll be gone in time

my creativity, my mind,
will still live on
in words i write

future generations
will read and understand
my thoughts, my soul

after i'm dead
i'll still be here

**the last conversation**

standing at the foot of the bed
our children on each side
we gathered to say goodbye

we met decades ago as teens-
in that instant, we knew
we were meant for each other

she talks to me with her eyes

i understand what she is saying,
her words speak to me as a tear on her face


i felt it
   slowly
      drip down
         my cheek

**tragedy today**

sitting on a park bench
alone as an old man,
looking at children
scamper on the grass-
i wonder what i might
say if my child
sat next to me today

after high school
he was drafted
into the army
during the '70s,
then sent overseas

he died in some jungle
in the middle of nowhere
meeting his destiny
i pray not in agony

now like then
old men send our
youth to battle

a leader born
with a silver spoon,
a bone spur deferment
and his kids flying
all over the world
killing endangered species,
he is sending out
our youth of today-
also an endangered species

**thinking**

today i sit on my patio
on a warm summer day,
overlooking a golf course,
the smell of fresh-cut grass
brings a flood of memories
roaring back

to being
a five-year-old
walking
the farmer's field
early morning;
smelling sweetness
of the warm dew
as tall grass
brush against
my bare legs

in the distance
cows stood silent,
watching
me sidestep
piles of cow chips;
avoiding the flies
swooping over them
with the day's heat
beginning to rise

as i walk back
to slide under
a barbed-wire fence,
ready to have breakfast
with my family
in the farm's

communal dining room,
i remember passing
the weather-beaten
planked barn,
doors always open,
hay from the loft
spewed
on the dirt floor,
spotting two large,
well-fed cats
lounging about,
indifferent
to my being there

now I'm waiting to die,
waiting to meet my parents again,
waiting to meet my maker, maybe

**America, the best country in the world**

i always believed
America is
the best country
in the world.
i grew up
saluting its flag,
proud of it, singing
the national anthem;
feeling secure when i travel
in any state because
i am an American

today i believe
America is filled
with bigotry,
racism,
hate speech,
military guns which kill
children in schools,
husband and wives,
mothers and fathers,
and young adults
in public places
robbed of their future

sadly, i wonder if
America is still the best
country in the world

i feel lost
and abandoned
in my America

**forgiveness**

unlock your heart
let the love in
hate out

live
love
bury hate
before it kills you

too many days wasted
not enough left to live,
embrace others' hearts
as many as you can

life and beauty
are finite,
love is not,
embrace it

**waiting for tomorrow**

the fan is turning so fast
above my head
as i lay in bed,
it looks to be a spinning wheel,
pushing air down, cooling us

draping her arm over my chest
with both our legs intertwined,
i never want it to end;
though i know, soon  it will

tomorrow's surgery
will be fifty-fifty,
the nodule
will be benign

we made it to retirement.

i always thought we would
be in Florida together,
however, it may not be-
will we sit on a beach
overlooking the ocean,
saltwater breezes
misting my tan face,
sipping a cold Piña Colada
on a balcony, high above the sand

lying here
waiting for tomorrow,
i think of what might
have been, yet still may

**desire**

standing four rows
behind her
during a service,
i notice
her hourglass shape
in a form-fitting
knit dress,
hair flowing
down her body,
sending me
back decades
to when i stood silent,
as a five-year-old
in a candy store
in 1950 Brooklyn-
drooling
at chocolate bars
ensconced
behind sliding
glass doors,
within my short reach,
yet miles away;
untouchable

**dreaming**

sometimes my thoughts drift
where the wind takes them,
carrying my heart along
to experience joy,
or bottomless despair;
not leaving me empty
or full, mixed feelings, yet
i continue on my path
on new adventures
every time the sun
goes down,
eyes close,
freeing my mind
to wander 'bout

**first time i saw you**

the first time
i saw you
standing there,
my heart sang out,
the world bloomed
without warning;
i heard birds sing,
rainbow-colored
butterflies fluttered,
red roses unfolded,
Bees buzzed about

my legs turned to jelly,
my speech impaired,
desire filled my mind

i did not know where to begin;
yet it came to me
as i look back on our lives,
these many decades later

i still see beauty,
i still feel love,
i still am crazy
about you

in my heart forever

**real people**

watching awards shows
i see a lot of people,
not normal folks
but show biz stars

perfect teeth,
white, lined up
in perfect rows
with frozen smiles

clothes more costly
then some cars,
bodies tailored
perfectly chiseled

we pay for them a
few bucks at a time,
good for them
they worked for it

not a cakewalk-
i don't want their money,
just their bodies
with great white teeth

## Susan

The casket swayed on the straps
Waiting for the priest to finish,
While three men stood motionless,
Each remembering Susan in their mind

Then workers loosen the winch
As she goes down one last time,
Alone, without the men on top
As they did for decades

While teenagers they loved her-
As a group, or all alone,
She was always one of them,
Every summer for years

At seventeen she went to
Confession once, never again;
The priest kept her for hours
In his office, shocked, amazed

They all married, Susan too,
Yet they still loved together
Now and then, for years-
Until her breast cancer canceled it

Close lifelong friends, hard to find,
Hard to keep, yet they all did.
Teen love can live forever,
Till death do us part

**Susan's sister**

we were teenagers in the sixties,
guys hanging out in the summertime
at two sisters' home on a lake,
we swam and fooled around

her younger sister liked my friend
but he was into older girls,
who were more mature and drove cars,
ignoring a cute girl, i did not

one day a whispered in her ear,
i had an instant camera,
if i took nude pictures of her
he might change his mind and date her

the next day i came back alone
with my parent's camera and film-
i spent the afternoon taking playboy
like pictures, helping her to find love

he never saw her naked pictures
because he was not interested;
although i am proud of the fact
i tried to help both of my friends

**at the library**

as i left after a meeting, such a bore,
a young girl, for me, held the door.
*my mind is younger than you think*
i said to her with a smile and a wink

an older man is what you see-
i look in a mirror; it is not me.
my mind is stuck in decades ago,
my legs and body now only go slow

at seventeen, you would have been mine,
at seventy-four, it's considered a crime.
all i can do is look and admire,
nothing else because i do tire

yet my thoughts run young and wild-
in my eyes, you're still a child.
lovely to look at, not to touch,
at my age, you are too much

off i go to sit and write
dream about what a sight.
you stir my mind, give it light,
today was just a pure delight

**eggs**

early one morning
there is an egg,
round and white
with a big yellow eye

she asked me
to eat it right,
with a fork and bread,
i said maybe tonight-
cause eggs
that are runny
don't sit well
in my tummy

i like mine
hard-boiled,
cut in half,
sprinkled with salt,
firm yellow yoke
held by fingers
then chewed,
swallowed,
or sometimes
mashed with mayo
on a soft Miami onion roll-
Ummm good

**confusion**

don't know why i didn't-
so many in the past,
blonds,
brunettes,
redheads,
big, small,
tall, short,
thin, heavy,
some beautiful
some models

back then, i failed
to choose one
over the others,
running around
fooling around
having my fun,
there were too many

all shapes
all sizes,
some nice,
some not,
some for friendship
some for fun-ship

there was no one
'till i met you,
then i underwent
total clarity

**her**

looking forward
i think back,
cupping my hands
holding your face
close to mine

a kiss
so tender
time stood still,
the earth stopped
stars became brighter,
my heartbeat stronger,
my legs felt like rubber

thinking back,
i now look forward
to reality

the future is imminent,
declared starkly,
truth,
no holds barred;
tomorrow
i face
the unthinkable

No!

**goodbye**

i saw a whale
breach the rough seas
of the North Atlantic,
shooting plumes of mist
high in the air,
then dive deep
flipping a tail
goodbye

i saw you
breach his heart,
an argument
between lovers
spewing
in the air
harsh words
to each other,
then you left,
flipping him
the bird
goodbye

**replaying life**

> floating down
> a river of memories,
> splashes of fond times
> flood my mind,
> soaking my body
> with warm feelings,
> ignoring the waterfall
> where the river soon ends

**undying love**

       you laid your face
       on my pillow;
       with tenderness
       you wrapped your arm
       over me, your thigh
       hugged mine,
       my heart flew to heaven

       life could not get any better

       you lit the flame
       of passion;
       unbounded love,
       flowing like the
       Niagara River
       rushing to the
       great falls-
       unstoppable force
       not to be trifled with
       or course changed

       when you left me
       for another
       with no notice,
       no goodbye,
       no note-
       my fragile soul
       shattered in pieces

       i miss you so much-
       there is not enough water
       in a great river to extinguish
       my flame for you

**karma**

    she ravaged my heart
    the way Boudica
    destroyed Rome's legions,
    with vengeance,
    malice, and
    bloodthirsty lust-
    only to have her
    cruelty mirrored
    by her next lover

**fidelity**

the band
ceased playing-
yet we still danced
in each other's arms

we never heard them stop

your head
nestled
by my cheek
i softly
kissed your neck,
holding you
in my arms
while the world
stopped
for us

we met
on a blind date
many decades ago

i'm still holding
you in my arms;
as you take
your last
breath of life

**the gift**

today
is my granddaughter's birthday-
the cake has five
burning candles;
our whole family
is sitting by the
table watching, as
she huffs and puffs
at the flickering yellow flames

i gave her a glass jar,
empty, wrapped in
white paper for her
to capture today's love-
little eyes open wide
when i said this is
a special gift

now she can keep
all the happiness
of her fifth birthday
forever in her mind;
whenever the cap
comes off,
then closes
her eyes to remember

**God**

    where is God?
    where can you find God?

    when children are crying
    ribs sticking out from hunger
    illness thirsting for more victims
    people living on the streets
    families in cardboard boxes
    digging through garbage cans
    for discarded food

    God stands for
    charity,
    hope,
    salvation,
    goodness,
    empathy,
    kindness

    *inside, we are all God*

    the problem is
    we do not
    knowingly
    acknowledge
    this fact,
    or act on it

**winter day in the cemetery**

    the winter wind is harsh-
    blasting my cheeks apple red
    with blistering force, while I
    glance to the lonely grave
    only yards away,
    a solitary stone
    in the middle of a field
    marking the eternal home
    of a beloved young girl

    life is so precious and short;
    we stumble along its path
    thinking we are in control,
    yet an unseen future
    plays with us,
    toys with us,
    and fools us
    into thinking
    it will never end,
    until it does

**happy new year**

      i welcome the new year,
      yet tears fall from my eyes;
      remembering those who
      died, fell ill, not healing,
      suffering in silence
      for my benefit

      life is to be cherished

      i do not understand
      cruelty,
      indifference to suffering
      by those with political power-
      our power;
      to help us,
      or those worse off

**the big question**

how can i laugh again
after the tears stop flowing?

my sadness
is unbearable;
moving on is hard

someday my time too
will arrive,
the problem is
i don't know when

who will cry for me?
was my life wasted?
did i make a difference?

is living
day after day
futile,
ending in
forever

will there be a
memory of
my ever being
here?

## the waitress

>her shift started
>early morning;
>with aching legs,
>fallen arches,
>trying to keep
>tired eyes open
>
>years ago
>her husband left;
>two young kids,
>gambling debts,
>hers to pay
>it's just the way,
>she has no say
>
>on a break
>she slouches
>in the back
>of her car,
>tinted windows,
>inhales a line-
>quick energy;
>needs to finish
>her shift this way
>
>no tomorrows
>just today, one
>more hour to go,
>then home to start
>over again,
>in the morning

***give me your tired, your poor***

in Denver-
five years old,
hungry, crying,
tears gushing,
eyes filled,
looking for
its mother
as she runs
to heat a bottle
for her baby-
a young child
craving food,
tenderness,
a mom's love

a similar child
on the border
is now caged,
still hungry,
all alone,
missing mom
because it's
skin is brown,
***yearning to breathe free***

*Welcome to Donald Trumps America*

**rain**

the drizzle changed
to a torrent
soaking everyone
waiting for the bus

standing in the aisle
between rows of seats
i held on
while the bus
rocked side to side
as it sped away

i noticed her seated
by the window, her blouse
drenched, clinging to her body
revealing feminine curves

our eyes met
we smiled-
silently, she said
***hello*** with pursed lips
and winked at me

we never spoke,
then left at the last stop
we walked our separate ways

for years we enjoyed an affair,
our spouses never knew;
then i awake each dawn from dreams
to catch another bus to work

**missing but here**

the early years are missing;
drugs and booze stole them
leaving a socially awkward
body with no memories at all

twenty-plus years of stupor
sleepwalking through life
with endless years in rehabs
till awakened at age forty

a twelve-step program did it
going to meetings every day-
the past is finally gone,
never lived nor experienced

it is the same body, just older,
but a mind still juvenile
not matured and seasoned,
now feeling its way in life

**sheep**

a herd mentality
rules the nation-
an unstable leader
makes secret deals
no witness or recordings
for history to know,
interpreter's notes are
confiscated,
then destroyed

maybe treason
maybe not,
no one now knows

in years to come
secrets always
leak out;
like a hidden
pregnancy,
the end is usually
a surprise for most-
yet sheep will always
follow,
unquestioning,
to their demise

**flight to Las Vegas**

engines roared with flaps extended-
my seatbelt tight the back upright
while overhead the cases shift
looking out, the plane did lift

down below the city looks small
even high buildings are not so tall
when looking down from up so high
i'm not afraid, yet i begin to sigh;
with the knowledge, we are going so fast
i pray our fuel will hold and last

hours away my plane will land
the flight attendants are so nice;
they pat my shoulder hold my hand,
cleaning up they scurry like mice

with a thump and a bump
the wheels touch down-
i say goodbye to my hosts today;
also, my money when i start to play

**Pearl**

paid by the hour,
maybe by the need-
working all night long
for addiction, she has to feed

it was a typical call,
a request for her time,
did she do out-calls
or only in-house

it has been years
since she went on her own.
no safety net pimp or madam
for protection, only her wits
with nerves of steel

the money is good,
her place in the rear
offers privacy,
a sense of security

one day the landlord
smelled an odor
by her apartment door,
he called the police

Pearl is dead-
her security oyster trashed,
destroyed; no one ever knew
her real name, another
nameless soul lost to drugs

**music**

    why did they
    play our tune
    on the radio after
    so many years passed

    nobody plays it anymore;
    too outdated, like us-
    we fell in love
    holding hands
    listening to our song

    like the music,
    my love
    for you
    never waned,
    always enjoyed

    it still brings,
    as you do,
    a smile to my heart

**the tree in my yard**

       i thought it strange
       the mighty tree
       in my yard has
       branches barren
       this summer

       year after year
       it blossomed
       in spring;
       reaching out
       with thick arms
       in all directions
       leaving piles
       of leaves
       for me to rake
       in chilly fall

       its trunk
       is massive
       decades
       in the making
       its strength
       sapped with age-
       we both have more
       in common now
       than i ever
       thought we did

## humanity

there are deranged people
who love with passion,
kill with lust,
sing with joy,
abuse with ease,
see alcohol then
drive blind drunk,
remember to pray
then forget the prayers,
God forgives them
or seeks retribution

the question becomes
not is God good or bad,
but why believe?

**my muse**

        how long
        do you carry
        a burning candle
        while the wax
        drips down,
        burning you,
        exposing the wick
        as it disappears
        into smoke,
        until finally
        in the end
        there is nothing
        but death
        for the flickering flame

        how long do you carry
        love in your heart
        as the years fly by,
        kicking yourself
        exposing heartbreak,
        it hurts until
        your final hours
        ending
        the torment

**driving to work**

      i saw a dog on the ground
      by the side of the street;
      broken, bruised,
      blood dried
      on its mouth
      no longer
      playing fetch

      lifeless,
      still,
      crows overhead
      a needless death

      somebody
      somewhere
      is missing
      a loving friend

**common emotions**

the bar starts
to fill
as she enters,
sitting at an empty stool,
eyes bloodshot
from crying

nursing a beer
she drinks another
shot of whiskey
tilting her head back
swishing it 'round
then swallowing

the love of her life
left for another woman
after ten years
of marriage; boilermakers
hardly drown the pain

love can hurt,
life's not fair,
this pain is far worse,
more humiliating
then years ago
when she came out
as a lesbian;
now shes sitting alone
in a happening club
surrounded by strangers,
who are trying to find
the love she thought she had

**finally, love**

at long last,
her gentle hand
held the back
of my head

she leaned in
placing soft
welcoming lips
against mine,
pursed,
tenderness
so wonderful;
sending sensations
i never felt before
throbbing
through my body

with eyes closed
my heart opened,
blinding me to
skin color,
never seeing it again;
we held
each other
in our arms,
and forever
in our hearts

**suicide**

when i look
at pictures
of the sun
on a horizon,
i wonder, is it
setting or rising?

the answer
depends on
my feelings
at the time

do i live
or end it?

so far, it is
always rising

**Other books of poetry by Elliot M. Rubin**

Scrambled Poems from my Heart
A Boutique Bouquet of Poems and Stories
Rumblings of an Old Man
Surf Avenue Girl - semi episodic poetry
Flash Pan Poetry
Unrequited Love
Aliyah - an Episodic Memoir
My Life if I took a Different Path -
    an Episodic Memoire
Bent Twigs and Wet Feet
Stories of the South
Selected Poems by Elliot M. Rubin

www.CreativeFiction.net